Praise for
Seven Day Anger Free Challenge

"Thinking you don't have anger issues? Read this book and think again. In a society that so easily excuses everything from irritability to outrage, *Seven Day Anger Free Challenge: Be the Peace* is a masterpiece. It quickly brings you from conviction to behavior transformation. I highly recommend this book as a personal development tool and gift to challenge others!"

~ *Kim M. Clark, multiple-award-winning author, publisher of Deep Waters Books, and nonprofit founder of Lift Your Gaze*

"This book is a call to everyone—a true challenge to consider how we view our own propensity for anger. Jacquelyn Lynn has provided a wonderful tool with ample scriptural footing to help us identify and avoid the triggers to unholy life responses."

~ *Mike Gilland, Operations Manager and host of "Afternoons With Mike," The Shepherd Radio Network*

"Jacquelyn Lynn not only presents the potentially life-changing *Seven Day Anger Free Challenge*, she also builds a foundation for success. Readers learn how to create a plan of action, create an anger trigger log, and keep a journal that includes excellent daily reflection questions. Jacquelyn is obviously passionate about helping readers complete their first challenge and continue to be the peace."

~ Gail Porter, author of
Will the Real Person Please Stand Up?

"You definitely won't get angry for investing the time to read *Seven Day Anger Free Challenge*. As with her other works, Jacquelyn Lynn provides us with positive solutions to everyday struggles."

~ Mark Goldstein, Central Florida Area Director, Christ Led Communities

"If you don't enjoy being angry, this book is for you! Anger is an unpleasant emotion, and this book directly offers helpful ways to control how we choose to respond to our environment. Fury often ignites in an instant, yet sometimes we later realize that the issue did not warrant such a reaction. The book of James warns us that "everyone should be quick to listen, slow to speak and slow to become angry." *Seven Day Anger Free Challenge* references that verse and lays out a plan to attain just that."

~Reverend Drew Marshall, PastorDrew.com

Seven Day Anger Free Challenge

Also by Jacquelyn Lynn

Choices (A Joyful Cup Story)

Finding Joy in the Morning: You can make it through the night

Words to Work By: 31 devotions for the workplace based on the Book of Proverbs

The Simple Facts About Self-Publishing: What indie publishers need to know to produce a great book

Work as Worship: How Your Labor Becomes Your Legacy

How to Survive an Active Shooter: What You do Before, During and After an Attack Could Save Your Life

Faith Words: Color the Words that Inspire You Every Day

Christian Meditations

Seven Day ANGER Free CHALLENGE

Be the Peace

Jacquelyn Lynn

The Seven Day Anger Free Challenge: Be the Peace
Copyright © 2021 by Jacquelyn Lynn

Cover design: Jerry D. Clement
Interior design & production: Tuscawilla Creative Services

All rights reserved. No part of this publication may be reproduced, distributed or transmitted in any form or by any means, without prior written permission, except in the case of brief quotations embodied in critical reviews and certain other noncommercial uses permitted by copyright law. Send permission requests to Permissions Coordinator at info@contacttcs.com.

Scripture quotations are taken from the Holy Bible, New Living Translation, copyright ©1996, 2004, 2015 by Tyndale House Foundation. Used by permission of Tyndale House Publishers, Carol Stream, Illinois 60188. All rights reserved.

Tuscawilla Creative Services • Winter Springs, FL USA
CreateTeachInspire.com

For bulk orders, contact info@contacttcs.com.

This publication is designed to provide accurate and authoritative information in regard to the subject matter covered. It is sold with the understanding that the publisher is not engaged in rendering legal, accounting, healthcare, or other professional services. If expert assistance is required, the services of a competent professional should be sought.

Library of Congress Control Number: 2021913437

ISBN: 978-1-941826-42-3 Hardback
978-1-941826-41-6 Paperback
978-1-941826-43-0 Ebook

*In memory of
Helen Morris Kearce*

CONTENTS

	The Story Behind the Anger Free Challenge	11
	The Anger Free Prayer	13
1	A Week Without Anger	15
2	The Impact of Anger	19
3	What God Says About Anger	27
4	A World Without Anger	31
5	Accept the Anger Free Challenge	33
6	When You've Completed the Challenge	37
	Anger Trigger Log	39
	Journal	45

THE STORY BEHIND THE ANGER FREE CHALLENGE

The Seven Day Anger Free Challenge began as an idea for a social media meme. As I thought about the message and how to design it into an image, I realized it was too much for a simple meme.

So I decided to write a blog. That didn't work, either. While I could get the core message into a 600-word article, there was more I wanted to say.

Before I knew it, I was writing a book.

But it's a short book. You can read the main message in less than a half-hour.

Although I could have made this book much longer, I didn't because I wanted it to be a quick read. My goal is for you to have enough information to make a decision about this life-changing challenge and, if you decide to accept it, to have a plan for implementation.

Are you ready?

Jacquelyn Lynn

THE ANGER FREE PRAYER

Help me to recognize situations that trigger my anger before I get angry.

Give me the strength I need to respond to anger triggers with peace, forgiveness, and love.

Make me better so that I may make the world around me better.

CHAPTER ONE

A WEEK WITHOUT ANGER

What would your life look like if you went a week without getting angry?

Just a week. Seven days of being anger free.

Imagine it: A week of not yelling at the kids, not cursing other drivers, not participating in ugly social media exchanges. Seven full days of not feeling upset or annoyed. One hundred sixty-eight consecutive hours of not having to apologize for something you said or did in anger.

Does that appeal to you? If so, you're ready for the Seven Day Anger Free Challenge—the challenge of going a week without getting angry.

I'm not talking about a week of not *expressing* your anger.

Most of us know how to be angry without expressing it. We've learned how to manage those feelings when we have to. We can smile and nod when our boss says something insulting or a customer does something that makes us mad. We can swallow a retort when a spouse, friend, or coworker irritates us over and over. We're still angry; we just don't show it—which means we're not anger free.

> *"Anger doesn't solve anything. It builds nothing, but it can destroy everything."*
> *– Thomas S. Monson*

I'm talking about a week of actually not *being* angry.

And I'm not the one challenging you to do it. This isn't an updated goofy social media challenge designed to raise money or awareness or prove that you read your friends' posts. It's not a contest or competition. It's a personal development exercise that will probably test you in more ways than you can imagine. It's something you will challenge yourself to do—and if you do that, if you work through the process, your life and the lives of everyone around you will be richer and more rewarding.

WHAT ARE YOU GIVING UP?

Anger is a powerful, controlling emotion that can trigger significant physical and psychological responses. The costs and consequences of anger are substantial. If you accept the Anger Free Challenge, what will you be giving up?

You'll be giving up strong feelings of annoyance, displeasure, and hostility—along with regret for how those feelings make you behave. You'll be giving up the potential of your anger escalating into rage. You'll be giving up the damage that anger does to your mind and body.

More important is what you'll be gaining when you're free of anger: peace, improved relationships, better health, greater productivity, and so much more.

CHAPTER TWO

Be the Peace

THE IMPACT OF ANGER

Freeing yourself from anger begins with understanding this intense emotion.

We don't go from calm to angry in one step. Anger is almost always driven by other feelings. Often our anger is visible but the cause of it isn't.

Before we get angry, we might feel frightened—fear is a common cause of anger. Other precursors to anger include humiliation, rejection, and betrayal. Or we might feel offended or hurt, or perhaps trapped.

A wide range of emotions can move us toward anger.

Anger triggers the body's "fight or flight" response, which is a survival mechanism designed to help us respond to danger, not anger. The adrenal glands flood the body with stress hormones and the brain shunts blood toward the muscles in preparation for physical exertion. Body temperature rises as heart rate, blood pressure, and respiration increase. While these reactions are helpful if you're in a dangerous situation, they can eventually take a toll on your mental and physical health if they're happening frequently. Short- and long-term health problems linked to anger include:

- Digestive issues
- Headaches
- Insomnia
- Anxiety
- High blood pressure
- Depression
- Heart attack
- Stroke

More importantly, anger can cause us to say and do things that hurt others and damage our relationships. It clouds our judgment and fuels bitterness. It distracts us and reduces our productivity. It distorts the truth. And in extreme situations, it can drive behavior that is dangerous and destructive.

The solution is to identify our anger triggers and deal with them *before* we get angry. It really is that simple—but it isn't easy. It's what makes the Anger Free Challenge so challenging but also so rewarding.

> *"Anger is an acid that can do more harm to the vessel in which it is stored than to anything on which it is poured."*
> – *Mark Twain*

What triggers your anger? It might be driving in heavy traffic and dealing with aggressive drivers. It might be your kids leaving their rooms in a mess. It might be your boss making unrealistic demands on your time. It might be a partner who betrays you or a coworker who takes advantage of you. It might be something as simple as the way another member of your household loads the dishwasher or where a neighbor leaves their trash bin. All of these situations begin with negative emotions, but they don't have to end in anger.

Here are some ways to keep negative emotions from escalating into anger:

Recognize the warning signs that you're about to get angry. Anger typically begins with feelings of annoyance and irritation. When you're getting annoyed, look for ways to either change the situation or remove yourself from it. If you can't do either of those, try some relaxation techniques or positive self-talk. Take control over your precursors to anger.

Change your perspective. Angry people often think things are worse than they actually are. Before you get to that point, step back and be logical. Try replacing your negative view with a positive one. And if you can't make it completely positive, at least try for more reasonable.

> *"Anger is only one letter short of danger."*
> *– Eleanor Roosevelt*

Manage your expectations. Be realistic in what you expect from yourself and others. Don't make impossible demands that will only leave you frustrated and angry when they're not met. Often it's the disappointment from unmet expectations that hurts us and leads to anger.

Use relaxation techniques that work for you. Take slow, controlled, deep breaths. Visualize yourself in a relaxed place or situation. If you can, do progressive muscle relaxation, which is a technique where you tense and relax each muscle group, slowly working your way through your body.

Move. Go for a walk or a run. Do a yoga practice. Dance. Getting yourself in motion can help you decompress and burn off feelings that can grow into anger.

> *"There is no revenge so complete as forgiveness."*
> — *Josh Billings*

Communicate. Have a calm, rational conversation with the other person or people involved. Let them talk and listen to what they have to say. Consider your response carefully.

Turn it over to God. Pray and ask God to handle it, then let it go.

CAN ANGER BE POSITIVE?

Can anger be good? Is there such a thing as positive, productive anger? Some say yes, but I don't think so. When we're angry, we're not thinking clearly or rationally—what good can come from us when we're in that state?

I've heard people claim they were driven by anger to do something good. While that may be true, my question is this: If anger prompted you to take positive action, why did you have to wait until you got angry to correct a wrong? Couldn't you see the wrong and do something about it without getting angry?

> *"While seeking revenge, dig two graves – one for yourself."*
> *– Douglas Horton*

Being anger free doesn't mean you don't seek justice or want to correct wrongs or that you're willing to let others take advantage of you. Being anger free means that you are in control of your emotions and you respond to people and circumstances in a calm, reasonable manner.

THE LINK BETWEEN ANGER AND REVENGE

Anger often spurs the urge to retaliate. This is what typically happens in road rage situations. One driver does something that makes another driver mad, so that driver retaliates, the first driver responds, and the situation quickly escalates out of control.

Revenge is a destructive, often violent response to anger that rarely brings the satisfaction being sought. When you seek revenge, you are essentially trying to change the past, which is impossible. Revenge is an attempt to increase your own position by asserting dominance, and that never works.

Once anger and the desire for revenge has manifested, the solution is forgiveness. It's the best constructive solution to dealing with your feelings. Be the bigger person; forgive, let go, and accept the Anger Free Challenge.

CHAPTER 3

Be the Peace

WHAT GOD SAYS ABOUT ANGER

Even though God is loving and merciful, the Bible has many references to times when people and nations felt God's wrath. Even Jesus appeared to display anger on occasion—most memorably when he drove the moneychangers out of the temple.

But God's anger is not the same as human anger. God's anger is always righteous, under control, and planned. And God is always quick to forgive when the target of his fury repents.

What does God say about anger in people?

The Bible clearly tells us that we are to avoid getting angry and associating with those who do, because nothing good can come from anger.

> *Stop being angry! Turn from your rage! Do not lose your temper—it only leads to harm. (Psalm 37:8)*
>
> *A hot-tempered person starts fights; a cool-tempered person stops them. (Proverbs 15:18)*
>
> *Don't befriend angry people or associate with hot-tempered people, or you will learn to be like them and endanger your soul. (Proverbs 22:24-25)*
>
> *Control your temper, for anger labels you a fool. (Ecclesiastes 7:9)*

In the Sermon on the Mount, Jesus warned against being angry.

> *"You have heard that our ancestors were told, 'You must not murder. If you commit murder, you are subject to judgment.' But I say, if you are even angry with someone,*

you are subject to judgment! If you call someone an idiot, you are in danger of being brought before the court. And if you curse someone, you are in danger of the fires of hell. (Matthew 5:21-22)

Various other New Testament passages tell us to avoid anger.

But now is the time to get rid of anger, rage, malicious behavior, slander, and dirty language. (Colossians 3:8)

In every place of worship, I want men to pray with holy hands lifted up to God, free from anger and controversy. (1 Timothy 2:8)

Understand this, my dear brothers and sisters: You must all be quick to listen, slow to speak, and slow to get angry. Human anger does not produce the righteousness God desires. (James 1:19-20)

In the previous chapter, we discussed practical reasons to avoid anger. If those aren't enough, consider this spiritual one: God does not want us to be angry.

CHAPTER FOUR

Be the Peace

A WORLD WITHOUT ANGER

What would life without anger be like?

On an individual level, it would mean not having those distressing feelings that drive our anger. We'd see our health improve as anger-related physical ailments disappear. We'd see our relationships improve as we deal with conflicts without losing our tempers and saying or doing hurtful things. We'd see our productivity improve because we're free to focus on positive things instead of the reason for and target of our anger.

Imagine that on a broader scale. Imagine the exponential effect people who have committed to be anger free could have on your community, your country, and even the world.

Is such a world possible? Probably not. That's why anger management has become an industry, and a book search on Amazon for "anger management" returns more than ten thousand results.

> *"To be angry is to revenge the faults of others on ourselves."*
> *– Alexander Pope*

But the Seven Day Anger Free Challenge isn't about changing the world. It's about changing you for seven days. Let's start there.

CHAPTER 5

ACCEPT THE ANGER FREE CHALLENGE

If you're ready to accept the Seven Day Anger Free Challenge, I'm excited for you. But before you start, you need a plan.

YOUR SEVEN DAY ANGER FREE PLAN

1. Make the commitment. Write it down, say it out loud: "I am going to be anger free for seven days." Whether you choose to share it with anyone else is up to you, but it's essential for your heart and mind to understand what you're doing.

2. Identify your anger triggers. Dig deep for this. Write them down; you can use the log on page 39. It may take some introspection and time for you to list all your triggers, but it's important that you know what they are so you can avoid them or at least manage them. Traffic is a common anger trigger. Long lines in stores is another. Your anger may be triggered by something a member of your household does or doesn't do, or by behaviors of people you work with. It may be triggered by social media posts or comments by political pundits. It's okay if some of your anger triggers seem petty—we've all gotten angry at things that don't bother others or that aren't truly important. The point is you need to recognize and acknowledge your triggers if you're going to succeed at the Anger Free Challenge.

> *"Anger is never without a reason, but seldom with a good one."*
> *– Benjamin Franklin*

> *"Anger is as a stone cast into a wasp's nest."*
> *– Pope Paul VI*

3. Plan for how you will handle your triggers. If

you can avoid them, great. But you won't be able to avoid every trigger, so what will you do to stay anger free when you're faced with a situation that usually makes you angry? It's important

> *"You will not be punished for your anger, you will be punished by your anger."*
> *– Buddha*

to acknowledge and address your triggers—don't just suppress them or deny your feelings. In addition to your known triggers, be prepared for surprises. Have a plan for what you'll do if something totally unexpected makes you feel angry. Chapter 2 lists some things you can do to prevent negative feelings from escalating into anger.

4. Set a start date. It can be tomorrow, it can be two or three days in the future. If you need time to prepare, take it. The key is to know the official beginning of your Anger Free Challenge.

5. Keep a journal. The journal in this book is designed specifically for the Anger Free Challenge. It includes a place for you to make your daily commitment, prayers, and questions to help you record your experiences and progress. But any journal, or even a plain notebook, will do. The key is to get your thoughts and feelings written down every day.

6. Begin each day with your commitment statement. Say, "I am going to be anger free for seven days. So far, I have been anger free for [insert number] days and will be anger free for at least [insert number] more days."

7. Prepare for failure. You might fail in your first attempt—or even your second or third. That's okay. Figure out what happened and forgive yourself. Then either keep going or start over—just don't quit.

8. Reward your success. Give yourself credit for every day you remain anger free and celebrate when you complete the challenge.

CHAPTER SIX

Be the Peace

WHEN YOU'VE COMPLETED THE CHALLENGE

What happens with you've completed the Seven Day Anger Free Challenge? First, accept my heartfelt congratulations. What you've done isn't easy.

Take some time to reflect on what you've achieved. Did you get through the challenge on your first try? Did it take restarting? How do you feel about it? How is your life different? Have you experienced any physical changes? Have your relationships changed? In what way? Use your journal to record your thoughts and feelings.

> *"Mankind must remember that peace is not God's gift to his creatures; peace is our gift to each other."*
> – *Elie Wiesel*

But what now? You essentially have two choices: you can remain anger free and work the challenge every day, or you can go back to the way you used to be.

I hope you'll choose to remain anger free. Keep working the challenge every day.

Share it with friends. Spread the word so the Anger Free Challenge can change the world.

SEVEN DAY ANGER FREE CHALLENGE ANGER TRIGGER LOG

Be the Peace

What makes you angry?

List the actions and circumstances that make you angry.

_____
_____
_____
_____
_____
_____
_____
_____
_____
_____
_____
_____
_____
_____
_____
_____
_____
_____
_____
_____
_____
_____
_____
_____
_____
_____

Specific situations that made you angry:

Briefly list the date/time, place, people involved, what happened, how it was resolved.

_____
_____
_____
_____
_____
_____
_____
_____
_____
_____
_____
_____
_____
_____
_____
_____
_____
_____
_____
_____

SEVEN DAY ANGER FREE CHALLENGE JOURNAL

Be the Peace

HOW TO USE THIS JOURNAL

*B*egin each day with your commitment statement and a prayer. During the seven days of the Anger Free Challenge, your statement could look like this:

"I am going to be anger free for seven days. So far, I have been anger free for [insert number] days and will be anger free for at least [insert number] more days."

After you have successfully completed the challenge, modify your commitment statement based on a promise you make to yourself for that day.

Close each day by journaling your end of the day reflections and plan for the next day.

Do you need to start over? Do you want to keep going after your first seven days? This book includes two sets of Seven Day Anger Free journal pages for you to use or share.

_____

Day, Date

My Commitment for Today

_____
_____
_____
_____
_____
_____

Be the Peace

Prayer to Start the Day

Awesome and Merciful God,

    You have made your feelings about anger abundantly clear. I ask your blessing and protection as I embark on this Seven Day Anger Free Challenge. Help me recognize and deal with feelings and situations that could lead to anger before I become angry. Keep me strong and guide me. May all I do be to your glory.

Amen.

Anger Free Challenge

Reflections

How was today different from yesterday?

_____
_____
_____
_____
_____
_____
_____

What emotions did you experience that could have turned into anger?

_____
_____
_____
_____
_____
_____
_____
_____
_____

Be the Peace

What situations did you handle well? What could you have handled better?

___

Other reflections

___

Anger Free Challenge

My Plan for Tomorrow

_____
_____
_____
_____
_____
_____
_____
_____
_____
_____
_____
_____
_____
_____
_____
_____
_____
_____
_____
_____
_____
_____
_____

_____
Day, Date

My Commitment for Today

_____
_____
_____
_____
_____
_____

Be the Peace

Prayer to Start the Day

Loving God,

    Thank you for yesterday. Thank you for all I learned, for the challenges I overcame. I couldn't have done it alone. Please be with me today, guiding me and protecting me as I seek to be anger free. May I be grounded and rooted in your Word.

Amen.

Anger Free Challenge

Reflections

What did you learn about yourself today?

_____
_____
_____
_____
_____
_____
_____
_____

Whom did you pray for and why?

_____
_____
_____
_____
_____
_____
_____
_____
_____
_____
_____

Did you feel God helping you turn away from anger?

Other reflections

Anger Free Challenge

My Plan for Tomorrow

_____

Day, Date

My Commitment for Today

_____
_____
_____
_____
_____
_____

Be the Peace

Prayer to Start the Day

God of Peace,

    You created us in your image and allowed us to glimpse your glory in Christ. I am so grateful to be your child. Please help me be obedient to your Word and may my actions today make you smile.

Amen.

Anger Free Challenge

Reflections

What was your biggest challenge today?

_____
_____
_____
_____
_____
_____
_____
_____
_____

Who have you told about the Anger Free Challenge? What was their reaction?

_____
_____
_____
_____
_____
_____
_____
_____
_____

What techniques did you use to stop an anger trigger from escalating to anger?

_____
_____
_____
_____
_____
_____
_____
_____
_____
_____

Other reflections

_____
_____
_____
_____
_____
_____
_____
_____
_____

Anger Free Challenge

My Plan for Tomorrow

_____
Day, Date

My Commitment for Today

_____
_____
_____
_____
_____
_____

Be the Peace

Prayer to Start the Day

Great and Glorious God,

    I'm at the halfway mark of the Anger Free Challenge. Thank you for getting me this far. Please help me to continue to serve you, to continue to grow in discipleship and be a positive reflection of you.

Amen.

Anger Free Challenge

Reflections

How has the Anger Free Challenge made you feel so far?

_____
_____
_____
_____
_____
_____
_____
_____
_____

Does it seem like people are reacting to you differently than they did before?

_____
_____
_____
_____
_____
_____
_____
_____
_____

Be the Peace

What is the most meaningful thing that happened today?

_____
_____
_____
_____
_____
_____
_____
_____
_____
_____

Other reflections

_____
_____
_____
_____
_____
_____
_____
_____
_____
_____

Anger Free Challenge

My Plan for Tomorrow

Day, Date

My Commitment for Today

_____
_____
_____
_____
_____
_____

Be the Peace

Prayer to Start the Day

Forgiving and Gracious God,
    Every day is a new day, created by you and blessed by you. Thank you for forgiving me and for giving me this fresh start. You are faithful and your compassions are new every morning. Help me to be more like you and to hear you when you speak to me.

Amen.

Anger Free Challenge

Reflections

What permanent changes has the Anger Free Challenge made in your life?

_____
_____
_____
_____
_____
_____
_____
_____
_____

Are you better at dealing with your anger triggers than you were before?

_____
_____
_____
_____
_____
_____
_____
_____
_____
_____
_____

Be the Peace

In what situation did you feel God's presence, helping you with the Anger Free Challenge?

_____
_____
_____
_____
_____
_____
_____
_____
_____

Other reflections

_____
_____
_____
_____
_____
_____
_____
_____
_____

My Plan for Tomorrow

Day, Date

My Commitment for Today

_____
_____
_____
_____
_____
_____

Be the Peace

Prayer to Start the Day

Almighty God, Giver of Strength,

You promise to always be with us. When I didn't know what to do, you showed me. Your hand guides everything I do. Thank you. As I go through the day, help me to keep your Word in my heart.

Amen.

Anger Free Challenge

Reflections

What happened today that gave you strength?

_____
_____
_____
_____
_____
_____
_____
_____
_____

Were you able to help someone else deal with their anger? How did you do that?

_____
_____
_____
_____
_____
_____
_____
_____

Have any of your relationships changed significantly since you began the Anger Free Challenge? Which ones and how?

_____

_____

_____

_____

_____

_____

_____

_____

_____

Other reflections

_____

_____

_____

_____

_____

_____

_____

_____

_____

Anger Free Challenge

My Plan for Tomorrow

_____
Day, Date

My Commitment for Today

_____
_____
_____
_____
_____
_____

Be the Peace

Prayer to Start the Day

God of all Comfort,

On my final day of this amazing journey, I thank you for making it possible. Thank you for your unending love and support, for the times you caught me when I stumbled, for guiding me when I wasn't sure what to do. Help me to see you, know you, and follow you every day.

Amen.

Anger Free Challenge

Reflections

What happened today that made you feel good?

_____
_____
_____
_____
_____
_____
_____
_____
_____

How are you different now compared to a week ago?

_____
_____
_____
_____
_____
_____
_____
_____
_____

Be the Peace

What will you do tomorrow that's related to the Anger Free Challenge?

Other reflections

My Plan for Tomorrow

Congratulations on completing the Seven Day Anger Free Challenge!

Here's another set of Seven Day Anger Free Challenge journal pages for you to use to continue your anger free experience or to share with a friend. If you want more pages, check out the *Anger Free Challenge Journal*, available online and wherever fine books are sold.

_____
Day, Date

My Commitment for Today

_____
_____
_____
_____
_____
_____

Be the Peace

Prayer to Start the Day

Awesome and Merciful God,

You have made your feelings about anger abundantly clear. I ask your blessing and protection as I embark on this Seven Day Anger Free Challenge. Help me recognize and deal with feelings and situations that could lead to anger before I become angry. Keep me strong and guide me. May all I do be to your glory.

Amen.

Anger Free Challenge

Reflections

How was today different from yesterday?

_____
_____
_____
_____
_____
_____
_____
_____

What emotions did you experience that could have turned into anger?

_____
_____
_____
_____
_____
_____
_____
_____
_____
_____
_____

Be the Peace

What situations did you handle well? What could you have handled better?

___

Other reflections

___

My Plan for Tomorrow

_____

Day, Date

My Commitment for Today

_____
_____
_____
_____
_____
_____

Be the Peace

Prayer to Start the Day

Loving God,
    Thank you for yesterday. Thank you for all I learned, for the challenges I overcame. I couldn't have done it alone. Please be with me today, guiding me and protecting me as I seek to be anger free. May I be grounded and rooted in your Word.

Amen.

Anger Free Challenge

Reflections

What did you learn about yourself today?

_____
_____
_____
_____
_____
_____
_____
_____

Whom did you pray for and why?

_____
_____
_____
_____
_____
_____
_____
_____
_____
_____
_____

Did you feel God helping you turn away from anger?

Other reflections

Anger Free Challenge

My Plan for Tomorrow

Day, Date

My Commitment for Today

_____
_____
_____
_____
_____
_____

Be the Peace

Prayer to Start the Day

God of Peace,

    You created us in your image and allowed us to glimpse your glory in Christ. I am so grateful to be your child. Please help me be obedient to your Word and may my actions today make you smile.

Amen.

Anger Free Challenge

Reflections

What was your biggest challenge today?

_____
_____
_____
_____
_____
_____
_____
_____

Who have you told about the Anger Free Challenge? What was their reaction?

_____
_____
_____
_____
_____
_____
_____
_____
_____
_____

What techniques did you use to stop an anger trigger from escalating to anger?

___

Other reflections

___

Anger Free Challenge

My Plan for Tomorrow

_____
Day, Date

My Commitment for Today

_____
_____
_____
_____
_____
_____

Be the Peace

Prayer to Start the Day

Great and Glorious God,

    I'm at the halfway mark of the Anger Free Challenge. Thank you for getting me this far. Please help me to continue to serve you, to continue to grow in discipleship and be a positive reflection of you.

Amen.

Anger Free Challenge

Reflections

How has the Anger Free Challenge made you feel so far?

_____
_____
_____
_____
_____
_____
_____
_____
_____

Does it seem like people are reacting to you differently than they did before?

_____
_____
_____
_____
_____
_____
_____
_____
_____

Be the Peace

What is the most meaningful thing that happened today?

_____
_____
_____
_____
_____
_____
_____
_____
_____
_____

Other reflections

_____
_____
_____
_____
_____
_____
_____
_____
_____

Anger Free Challenge

My Plan for Tomorrow

_____
Day, Date

My Commitment for Today

_____
_____
_____
_____
_____
_____

Be the Peace

Prayer to Start the Day

Forgiving and Gracious God,

    Every day is a new day, created by you and blessed by you. Thank you for forgiving me and for giving me this fresh start. You are faithful and your compassions are new every morning. Help me to be more like you and to hear you when you speak to me.

Amen.

Anger Free Challenge

Reflections

What permanent changes has the Anger Free Challenge made in your life?

_____
_____
_____
_____
_____
_____
_____
_____
_____

Are you better at dealing with your anger triggers than you were before?

_____
_____
_____
_____
_____
_____
_____
_____
_____
_____
_____

In what situation did you feel God's presence, helping you with the Anger Free Challenge?

___

Other reflections

___

Anger Free Challenge

My Plan for Tomorrow

Day, Date

My Commitment for Today

_____
_____
_____
_____
_____
_____

Be the Peace

Prayer to Start the Day

Almighty God, Giver of Strength,

You promise to always be with us. When I didn't know what to do, you showed me. Your hand guides everything I do. Thank you. As I go through the day, help me to keep your Word in my heart.

Amen.

Anger Free Challenge

Reflections

What happened today that gave you strength?

_____
_____
_____
_____
_____
_____
_____
_____
_____

Were you able to help someone else deal with their anger? How did you do that?

_____
_____
_____
_____
_____
_____
_____
_____
_____

Be the Peace

Have any of your relationships changed significantly since you began the Anger Free Challenge? Which ones and how?

_____
_____
_____
_____
_____
_____
_____
_____
_____

Other reflections

_____
_____
_____
_____
_____
_____
_____
_____

Anger Free Challenge

My Plan for Tomorrow

_____
Day, Date

My Commitment for Today

_____
_____
_____
_____
_____
_____

Be the Peace

Prayer to Start the Day

God of all Comfort,

    On my final day of this amazing journey, I thank you for making it possible. Thank you for your unending love and support, for the times you caught me when I stumbled, for guiding me when I wasn't sure what to do. Help me to see you, know you, and follow you every day.

Amen.

Anger Free Challenge

Reflections

What happened today that made you feel good?

_____
_____
_____
_____
_____
_____
_____
_____
_____

How are you different now compared to a week ago?

_____
_____
_____
_____
_____
_____
_____
_____
_____

Be the Peace

What will you do tomorrow that's related to the Anger Free Challenge?

_____
_____
_____
_____
_____
_____
_____
_____
_____

Other reflections

_____
_____
_____
_____
_____
_____
_____
_____
_____

Anger Free Challenge

My Plan for Tomorrow

Congratulations on completing the Seven Day Anger Free Challenge.

If you want more pages, check out the *Anger Free Challenge Journal,* available online and wherever fine books are sold.

Jacquelyn Lynn finds joy in serving others through her writing.

Her more than 40 books include *Finding Joy in the Morning: You can make it through the night* (companion books: *Finding Joy Journal, Finding Joy Adult Coloring Book,* and *Intentional Joy Study Guide*); *Words to Work By: 31 devotions for the workplace based on the book of Proverbs*; and *Choices*, the first novel in the Joyful Cup Story series.

Jacquelyn is also the author of *The Simple Facts About Self-Publishing: What indie publishers need to know to produce a great book*. Jacquelyn partners with her husband, Jerry Clement, on their book projects as well as on ghostwriting and producing books for clients. Together they created two Christian coloring books for adults, *Christian Meditations* and *Faith Words*.

Visit **CreateTeachInspire.com** to learn more about Jacquelyn. You can sign up to receive her weekly inspirational messages and find links to connect with her on social media.

Continue Your Anger Free Journey

Featuring thought-provoking writing prompts, scripture, inspirational quotes, and more.

Available online or ask your favorite local bookstore to order it for you.

The Finding Joy Collection

Simple but powerful strategies to help you meet life's toughest challenges and find joy *every* morning.

Available online or order through your favorite local bookstore.

A single moment
The wrong choice
Lives change ...
forever.

Available on Amazon and wherever fine books are sold.

Color Your Faith

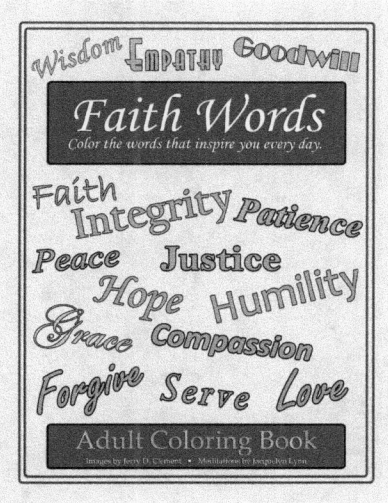

Available online or order through your favorite local bookstore.

Messages of inspiration and motivation based on the teachings of the world's greatest business advisor: King Solomon.

Devotions ideal for beginning your work day, opening a meeting, or just taking a break.

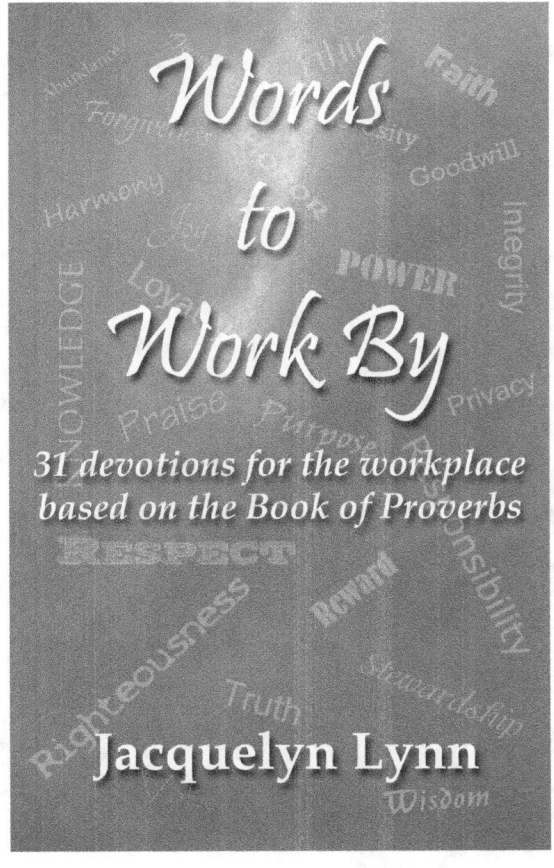

Available on Amazon and all online book retailers.

Is writing and publishing a book on your bucket list?

Find out what it takes to produce a quality book that will delight your audience and meet your goals.

Available online or order through your favorite local bookstore.

www.ingramcontent.com/pod-product-compliance
Lightning Source LLC
Chambersburg PA
CBHW072040110526
44592CB00012B/1498